Books by A. Poulin, Jr.

Saltimbanques; Prose Poems by Rainer Maria Rilke
(Translator)

The Widow's Taboo: Poems After the Catawba

Catawba: Omens, Prayers & Songs

Duino Elegies and Sonnets to Orpheus by Rainer Maria
Rilke (Translator)

In Advent: Poems

Contemporary American Poetry (Editor)

*The American Folk Scene: Dimensions of the Folksong
Revival* (Co-Editor with David A. DeTurk)

The Roses
&
The Windows

Rainer Maria Rilke

The Roses
&
The Windows

Translated from the French by

A. Poulin, Jr.

Foreword by

W. D. Snodgrass

Graywolf Press

I wish to thank the Research Foundation of the State University of New York for fellowships during which these translations were first started. I also wish to thank the State University of New York, College at Brockport, for a sabbatical during which these translations were completed. —A. Poulin, Jr.

The original French poems comprising these two sequences, *Les Roses* and *Les Fenêtres*, have been collected in Rainer Maria Rilke *Sämtliche Werke*, Zweiter Band, Gedichte: Zweiter Teil, Insel-Verlag, 1958.

ISBN 0-915308-21-5

First edition

Contents

Foreword

Ever since I first read Rilke's German poems, I knew he had also written poems in French. I assumed though (and many readers must share this misconception) that those were few and slight—like Eliot's French poems, more a language exercise than a serious effort at poetic creation. I am startled, now, to find that they run to nearly 400—enough to establish a significant career even had Rilke written nothing else. The two sequences from that corpus which A. Poulin, Jr. has chosen, here, to translate give warning that the French poems may also carry considerable weight and power.

According to Siegfried Mandel, Rilke had written only 28 French poems before 1922. In that year, of course, he was able to complete the *Duino Elegies*, the massive work that had remained unfinished through 10 years of terrible silence. As is well known, in the great release and outpouring of energy after the completion of his masterpiece, Rilke composed, in 18 days, all 56 of *The Sonnets to Orpheus*. According to Mandel, Rilke composed all of the rest of his French poems between this period and his death in 1926. So we must consider them also, I think, part of that triumphant overflow of celebration and praise; even the choice of the second language seems part of their joyous superfluity of creation. Like the rose in the first of these poems,

Rilke had found such repose and sleep in his own center, that his tendernesses could wake, "touch, converge into an urgent mouth."

In both style and subject, also, these poems are closely related to *The Sonnets to Orpheus*. They offer us all of Rilke's accustomed elegance of attitude, his grace of diction, above all his wealth and generosity of creation, that effortless heaping of image upon image, invention upon invention, loveliness upon loveliness. At times they seem so quintessentially Rilkean as to be downright unrepresentative.

And there *are* differences; unquestionably they are lighter, more joyous, more deft and playful. I cannot help wondering how much this coloring may be influenced by the different language; but perhaps it is merely that the fearful confrontation of the abyss has receded further into the past. In any case, these poems lack the muscularity, the monumental awkwardness of the *Elegies*, even of such shorter poems as "Orpheus, Eurydice, Hermes." Merely to mention their generosity is, perhaps, to admit that they are gratuitous, an unforced gift, not under the compulsion of Rilke's most profound creations. They are unnecessary, as were the *airs de cour* of the French Renaissance—small acts of unexacted delight at the accomplishment of an obligatory mission. Like the *airs*, they may seem to slip toward the precious if we forget the past struggle on which they are based.

Having himself faced the trial of translating the

Duino Elegies and *The Sonnets to Orpheus*, Poulin now turns, as Rilke himself did, to this poetry of bounty. There is an irony, here, however. Translating the *Sonnets* and the *Elegies*, Poulin was forced to sojourn in Rilke's native language, one alien to him. Translating *The Roses* and *The Windows* where Rilke leaves his native language, Poulin is restored to *his*. In any case, he has made available to those of us who read neither, a new and unsuspected wealth of joyous inventions; how could we be less than grateful!

W. D. Snodgrass
Norfolk, Va.
August 12, 1978

Les Roses

The Roses

This translation for Bertrand Mathieu

Rose, ô pure contradiction,
volupté de n'être le sommeil de personne
sous tant de paupières.
                              —R. M. Rilke

I

Si ta fraîcheur parfois nous étonne tant,
heureuse rose,
c'est qu'en toi-même, en dedans,
pétale contre pétale, tu te reposes.

Ensemble tout éveillé, dont le milieu
dort, pendant qu'innombrables, se touchent
les tendresses de ce cœur silencieux
qui aboutissent à l'extrême bouche.

I

If we're sometimes so amazed
by your freshness, happy rose,
it's that deep inside yourself,
petal against petal, you're in repose.

Fully awake while their center's slept
who knows how long, this silent
heart's tendernesses touch,
converge into an urgent mouth.

II

Je te vois, rose, livre entrebâillé,
qui contient tant de pages
de bonheur détaillé
qu'on ne lira jamais. Livre-mage,

qui s'ouvre au vent et qui peut être lu
les yeux fermés . . . ,
dont les papillons sortent confus
d'avoir eu les mêmes idées.

II

I see you, rose, half-open book
filled with so many pages
of that detailed happiness
we will never read. Magus-book,

opened by the wind and read
with our eyes closed . . . ,
butterflies fly out of you, stunned
for having had the same ideas.

III

Rose, toi, ô chose par excellence complète
qui se contient infiniment
et qui infiniment se répand, ô tête
d'un corps par trop de douceur absent,

rien ne te vaut, ô toi, suprême essence
de ce flottant séjour;
de cet espace d'amour où à peine l'on avance
ton parfum fait le tour.

III

Rose, O you completely perfect thing,
always self-contained and yet
spilling yourself forever—O head
of a torso with too much sweetness missing,

nothing's your equal, O you, supreme
essence of this fragile place;
your perfume is the very seam
of this love-space we barely penetrate.

IV

C'est pourtant nous qui t'avons proposé
de remplir ton calice.
Enchantée de cet artifice,
ton abondance l'avait osé.

Tu étais assez riche, pour devenir cent fois toi-même
en une seule fleur;
c'est l'état de celui qui aime . . .
Mais tu n'as pas pensé ailleurs.

IV

Surely it was us who encouraged
you to refill your calyx.
Enchanted by such artifice,
your abundance found its courage.

You were rich enough to be yourself
a hundred times in just one flower;
that's the condition of the lover . . .
But you never did think otherwise.

V

Abandon entouré d'abandon,
tendresse touchant aux tendresses . . .
C'est ton intérieur qui sans cesse
se caresse, dirait-on;

se caresse en soi-même,
par son propre reflet éclairé.
Ainsi tu inventes le thème
du Narcisse exaucé.

V

Abandon surrounds abandon,
tenderness touches tenderness . . .
You'd think your center would caress
itself on and on and on . . .

caress itself in itself and seem
to glow with its own image.
Thus you invent the theme
of the fulfilled Narcissus.

VI

Une rose seule, c'est toutes les roses
et celle-ci: l'irremplaçable,
le parfait, le souple vocable
encadré par le texte des choses.

Comment jamais dire sans elle
ce que furent nos espérances,
et les tendres intermittences
dans la partance continuelle.

VI

A single rose is every rose
and this one: irreplaceable,
perfect, a supple vocable
by the text of things enclosed.

Without her, how can we ever
talk about what our hopes were,
about the tender intervals
in this perpetual departure.

VII

T'appuyant, fraîche claire
rose, contre mon œil fermé—,
on dirait mille paupières
superposées

contre la mienne chaude.
Mille sommeils contre ma feinte
sous laquelle je rôde
dans l'odorant labyrinthe.

VII

Bright cool rose leaning
on my eye that's closed,
like a thousand eyelids
superimposed

on mine that's warm.
A thousand sleeps against
this counterfeit in which I roam
in a fragrant labyrinth.

VIII

De ton rêve trop plein,
fleur en dedans nombreuse,
mouillée comme une pleureuse,
tu te penches sur le matin.

Tes douces forces qui dorment,
dans un désir incertain,
développent ces tendres formes
entre joues et seins.

VIII

Overflowing with your dream,
flower with so many others deep
inside, wet as one who weeps,
you lean against the dawn.

In a precarious wish,
your gentle sleeping powers
shape those very tender
forms of cheeks and breasts.

Rose, toute ardente et pourtant claire,
que l'on devrait nommer reliquaire
de Sainte-Rose . . . , rose qui distribue
cette troublante odeur de sainte nue.

Rose plus jamais tentée, déconcertante
de son interne paix; ultime amante,
si loin d'Ève, de sa première alerte—,
rose qui infiniment possède la perte.

IX

Rose, so clear and yet so fiery
that we should call you reliquary
of Saint Rose . . . ; rose, you dispense
this troubling odor of a naked saint.

Rose never tempted again, disconcerter
by your inner peace; ultimate lover,
so far from Eve, from her first call—
rose infinitely holding the fall.

X

Amie des heures où aucun être ne reste,
où tout se refuse au cœur amer;
consolatrice dont la présence atteste
tant de caresses qui flottent dans l'air.

Si l'on renonce à vivre, si l'on renie
ce qui était et ce qui peut arriver,
pense-t-on jamais assez à l'insistante amie
qui à côté de nous fait son œuvre de fée.

X

Friend of hours when no one remains,
when all's refused to the bitter heart;
comforter whose presence attests
to such caresses floating in the air.

If we refuse to live, if we renounce
what was and what may happen still,
we never think enough of this tenacious friend
who's next to us, at work on miracles.

XI

J'ai une telle conscience de ton
être, rose complète,
que mon consentement te confond
avec mon cœur en fête.

Je te respire comme si tu étais,
rose, toute la vie,
et je me sens l'ami parfait
d'une telle amie.

XI

I'm so conscious of your being,
total rose,
my assent's confusing
you with my celebrating heart.

Rose, I breathe you in as if
you were all of life,
and I feel I am the perfect
friend of such a friend.

XII

Contre qui, rose,
avez-vous adopté
ces épines?
Votre joie trop fine
vous a-t-elle forcée
de devenir cette chose
armée?

Mais de qui vous protège
cette arme exagérée?
Combien d'ennemis vous ai-je
enlevés
qui ne la craignaient point.
Au contraire, d'été en automne,
vous blessez les soins
qu'on vous donne.

XII

Rose, against whom
did you assume
those thorns?
Did your too delicate
joy force you
to become that
armed thing?

But from whom does this
extravagant weapon protect
you? How many enemies
stole off with you
because they weren't afraid of it?
Instead, from summer to autumn
you wound the attention
that's poured over you.

XIII

Préfères-tu, rose, être l'ardente compagne
de nos transports présents?
Est-ce le souvenir qui davantage te gagne
lorsqu'un bonheur se reprend?

Tant de fois je t'ai vue, heureuse et sèche,
—chaque pétale un linceul—
dans un coffret odorant, à côté d'une mèche,
ou dans un livre aimé qu'on relira seul.

XIII

Rose, do you prefer to be the ardent friend
of our present ecstasy?
Or are you won over more by memory,
when one joy's relived again?

How often I have seen you, happy, parched
—each petal a shroud—
in a fragrant box, next to a match,
or in a favorite book re-read alone out loud.

XIV

Été: être pour quelques jours
le contemporain des roses;
respirer ce qui flotte autour
de leurs âmes écloses.

Faire de chacune qui se meurt
une confidante,
et survivre à cette sœur
en d'autres roses absente.

XIV

Summer: for a few days being
the contemporary of roses;
to breathe what's floating
around their hearts in bloom.

To make each dying one
a confidante,
and to survive this sister in
other roses that are absent.

XV

Seule, ô abondante fleur,
tu crées ton propre espace;
tu te mires dans une glace
d'odeur.

Ton parfum entoure comme d'autres pétales
ton innombrable calice.
Je te retiens, tu t'étales,
prodigieuse actrice.

XV

All alone, O abundant flower,
you create your own space;
you stare at yourself in a mirror
of odor.

Your fragrance swirls: more petals
around your teeming calyx.
I hold you back, you sprawl,
marvellous actress.

XVI

Ne parlons pas de toi. Tu es ineffable
selon ta nature.
D'autres fleurs ornent la table
que tu transfigures.

On te met dans un simple vase—,
voici que tout change:
c'est peut-être la même phrase,
mais chantée par un ange.

XVI

Let's not speak of you. Ineffable.
That is your nature.
Other flowers decorate the table
you transfigure.

We put you in a simple vase—
everything is mutable;
perhaps it's the same phrase,
but now sung by an angel.

XVII

C'est toi qui prépares en toi
plus que toi, ton ultime essence.
Ce qui sort de toi, ce troublant émoi,
c'est ta danse.

Chaque pétale consent
et fait dans le vent
quelques pas odorants
invisibles.

Ô musique des yeux,
toute entourée d'eux,
tu deviens au milieu
intangible.

XVII

It's you who in you is preparing
more than you: your ultimate essence.
The troubling motion emerging
out of you is your dance.

Each petal consents
and takes a few fragrant,
invisible
steps in the wind.

O music of eyes!
Completely circumscribed
by them, in their middle
you become intangible.

XVIII

Tout ce qui nous émeut, tu le partages.
Mais ce qui t'arrive, nous l'ignorons.
Il faudrait être cent papillons
pour lire toutes tes pages.

Il y en a d'entre vous qui sont comme des dictionnaires;
ceux qui les cueillent
ont envie de faire relier toutes ces feuilles.
Moi, j'aime les roses épistolaires.

XVIII

You're touched by all that touches us.
But whatever happens to you we ignore.
We'd have to be a hundred butterflies
to read all those pages of yours.

Some of you are like dictionaries;
people who are their collectors
have an urge to re-read all the entries.
I love roses that are letters.

XIX

Est-ce en exemple que tu te proposes?
Peut-on se remplir comme les roses,
en multipliant sa subtile matière
qu'on avait faite pour ne rien faire?

Car ce n'est pas travailler que d'être
une rose, dirait-on.
Dieu, en regardant par la fenêtre,
fait la maison.

XIX

Do you set yourself up as example?
Can we replenish our own subtle
matter like roses by multiplying
what we once did just to do nothing?

Because it really isn't work, you know,
just to be a rose.
God, while looking out a window,
picks up the house.

XX

Dis-moi, rose, d'où vient
qu'en toi-même enclose,
ta lente essence impose
à cet espace en prose
tous ces transports aériens?

Combien de fois cet air
prétend que les choses le trouent,
ou, avec une moue,
il se montre amer.
Tandis qu'autour de ta chair,
rose, il fait la roue.

XX

Except from your inner
circle, tell me, rose,
where does your slow essence
come from to impose
all those unearthly raptures
on this space of prose?

How often does this air
pretend that everything tears
it, or, with a scowl,
seems to be so bitter.
While around your petals,
rose, it swaggers.

XXI

Cela ne te donne-t-il pas le vertige
de tourner autour de toi sur ta tige
pour te terminer, rose ronde?
Mais quand ton propre élan t'inonde,

tu t'ignores dans ton bouton.
C'est un monde qui tourne en rond
pour que son calme centre ose
le rond repos de la ronde rose.

XXI

All that spinning on your stem
to end yourself, round rose,
doesn't that make you dizzy?
But drenched by your own impetus,

in your bud you just ignore
yourself. It's a world that whirls
around so its calm center dares
the round repose of the round rose.

XXII

Vous encore, vous sortez
de la terre des morts,
rose, vous qui portez
vers un jour tout en or

ce bonheur convaincu.
L'autorisent-ils, eux
dont la crâne creux
n'en a jamais tant su?

XXII

You again, you rising
out of the earth of the dead,
rose, you who are carrying
toward a day all in gold

this convincing happiness.
And those whose sunken
skulls have never known
so much, do they say yes?

XXIII

Rose, venue très tard, que les nuits amères arrêtent
par leur trop sidérale clarté,
rose, devines-tu les faciles délices complètes
de tes sœurs d'été?

Pendant des jours et des jours je te vois qui hésites
dans ta gaine serrée trop fort.
Rose qui, en naissant, à rebours imites
les lenteurs de la mort.

Ton innombrable état te fait-il connaître
dans un mélange où tout se confond,
cet ineffable accord du néant et de l'être
que nous ignorons?

XXIII

Late-blooming rose that the bitter
nights stop with their too sidereal light,
rose, do you suspect the easy full delights
of your summer sisters?

Day after day I watch you hesitate
in your sheath too tightly tied.
Rose who, being born, in reverse imitates
the slow ways of those who've died.

Does your endless state make you capable of knowing,
in some *mélange* where everything is fused,
that speechless harmony of nothingness and being
we so ignorantly refuse?

XXIV

Rose, terrestre pourtant, à nous autres égale,
fleur de toutes nos fleurs,
est-ce que tu sens en toi, pétale contre pétale,
nos palpables bonheurs.

Ces attouchements doux qui te remplissent, ô rose,
est-ce que leur somme comprend
tout ce qu'on avait osé, tout ce que l'on ose
et le plaisir hésitant?

XXIV

Rose, certainly earthly and our equal,
flower of all our flowers,
inside yourself, petal over petal, do you feel
our own palpable pleasures?

These tender touches filling you, O rose,
does their measure comprise
all that we've dared, all that we venture,
and this hesitant happiness?

XXV

Rose, à nos habitudes si chère,
à nos plus chers souvenirs dédiée,
devenue presque imaginaire
pour être tant à nos rêves liée—,

Rose qui, silencieuse, surpasse
en se mêlant à l'air, les chants,
qui triomphe dans la rosace
et qui meurt entre deux amants.

XXV

Rose, so cherished by our customs,
dedicated to our dearest memories,
become almost imaginary
for being so linked to our dreams—

silent while becoming air, rose
eclipsing all the canticles,
that is triumphant in the rose
window, and between two lovers dies.

XXVI

Infiniment rassurée
malgré tant de dangers
sans jamais rien changer
à ses habitudes,
la rose qui s'ouvre, prélude
à son innombrable durée.

Sait-on combien elle vit?
Un de ses jours, sans doute,
c'est toute la terre, toute
l'infinité d'ici.

XXVI

Infinitely at ease
despite so many risks,
with no variation
of her usual routine,
the blooming rose is the omen
of her immeasurable endurance.

Do we know how she survives?
No doubt one of her days
is all the earth and all
of our infinity.

XXVII

Rose, eût-il fallu te laisser dehors,
chère exquise?
Que fait une rose là où le sort
sur nous s'épuise?

Point de retour. Te voici
qui partages
avec nous, éperdue, cette vie, cette vie
qui n'est pas de ton âge.

XXVII

Rose, did you have to be left
outdoors, exquisite dear?
What is a rose doing here
where fate exhausts itself on us?

Point of no return. You're left
with us now, sharing,
desperately, this life, this life
where you don't belong.

Translator's Note

Most of these poems are part of Rilke's original sequence, *Les Roses*. However, poems XXIV, XXV and XXVI are from Rilke's notebooks (1921–1926) where they are grouped together under the French title "Roses."

Les Fenêtres

The Windows

This translation for Arthur Furst and Jeannea Paine

échantillon d'une liberté compromise
par la présence du sort;
prise par laquelle parmi nous s'égalise
le grand trop du dehors.
                    —R. M. Rilke

I

Il suffit que, sur un balcon
ou dans l'encadrement d'une fenêtre,
une femme hésite . . . , pour être
celle que nous perdons
en l'ayant vue apparaître.

Et si elle lève les bras
pour nouer ses cheveux, tendre vase:
combien notre perte par là
gagne soudain d'emphase
et notre malheur d'éclat!

I

It's enough that on a balcony
or in a window frame
a woman pauses . . . , to be
the one we lose
just by seeing her appear.

And if she lifts her arms
to tie her hair, tender vase:
how much our loss gains
a sudden emphasis,
our sadness brilliance!

II

Tu me proposes, fenêtre étrange, d'attendre;
déjà presque bouge ton rideau beige.
Devrais-je, ô fenêtre, à ton invite me rendre?
Ou me défendre, fenêtre? Qui attendrais-je?

Ne suis-je intact, avec cette vie qui écoute,
avec ce cœur tout plein que la perte complète?
Avec cette route qui passe devant, et le doute
que tu puisses donner ce trop dont le rêve m'arrête?

II

You propose I wait, strange window;
your beige curtain nearly billows.
O window, should I accept your offer or,
window, defend myself? Who would I wait for?

Aren't I intact, with this life that's listening,
with this full heart that loss is completing?
With this road running in front, and the qualm
you give this excess that stops me with its dream?

III

N'es-tu pas notre géométrie,
fenêtre, très simple forme
qui sans effort circonscris
notre vie énorme?

Celle qu'on aime n'est jamais plus belle
que lorsqu'on la voit apparaître
encadrée de toi; c'est, ô fenêtre,
que tu la rends presque éternelle.

Tous les hasards sont abolis. L'être
se tient au milieu de l'amour,
avec ce peu d'espace autour
dont on est maître.

III

Aren't you our geometry,
window, very simple shape
circumscribing our enormous
life painlessly?

A lover's never so beautiful
as when we see her appear
framed by you; because, window,
you make her almost immortal.

All risks are cancelled. Being
stands at love's center,
with this narrow space around,
where we are master.

IV

Fenètre, toi, ô mesure d'attente,
tant de fois remplie,
quand une vie se verse et s'impatiente
vers une autre vie.

Toi qui sépares et qui attires,
changeante comme la mer,—
glace, soudain, oú notre figure se mire
mêlée à ce qu'on voit à travers;

échantillon d'une liberté compromise
par la présence du sort;
prise par laquelle parmi nous s'égalise
le grand trop du dehors.

IV

You, window, O waiting's measure,
refilled so often
when one life spills out and grows
impatient for another.

You who divides and attracts,
as fickle as the sea—
sudden mirror reflecting our face
mingled with what we see in back;

fraction of a freedom compromised
by the presence of risk;
trapped by whatever's in us
that evens the odds of the loaded outside.

V

Comme tu ajoutes à tout,
fenêtre, le sens de nos rites:
quelqu'un qui ne serait que debout,
dans ton cadre attend ou médite.

Tel distrait, tel paresseux,
c'est toi qui le mets en page:
il se ressemble un peu,
il devient son image.

Perdu dans un vague ennui,
l'enfant s'y appuie et reste;
il rêve . . . Ce n'est pas lui,
c'est le temps qui use sa veste.

Et les amantes, les y voit-on,
immobiles et frêles,
percées comme les papillons
pour la beauté de leurs ailes.

V

Window, how you add the sense
of our rites to everything:
someone who is simply standing
waits or meditates inside your frame.

The one who's lazy or distracted
—you set him into motion:
he looks a little like himself,
he becomes his own reflection.

Lost in vague boredom,
a child leans on you and rests;
he dreams . . . It's not him,
it's time using his vest.

And look at all the loving,
motionless and fragile:
butterflies pinned
for their beautiful wings.

VI

Du fond de la chambre, du lit, ce n'était que pâleur qui sépare,
la fenêtre stellaire cédant à la fenêtre avare
qui proclame le jour.
Mais la voici qui accourt, qui se penche, qui reste:
après l'abandon de la nuit, cette neuve jeunesse céleste
consent à son tour!

Rien dans le ciel matinal que la tendre amante contemple,
rien que lui-même, ce ciel, immense exemple:
profondeur et hauteur!
Sauf les colombes qui font dans l'air de rondes arènes,
où leur vol allumé en douces courbes promène
un retour de douceur.

VI

From the back of the room, the bed, only a pallor spread,
    the starry window surrendering to the greedy window
        announcing the day.
But here comes the one who hurries, who leans, and stays:
after night's abandonment, it's this new and heavenly
        girl's turn to say yes!

At nothing else in the morning sky, the tender lover stares
    at nothing but the enormous example of the sky himself:
        the heights and depths!
Only doves making round arenas in the air,
where their flight flashing in soft arcs parades
        a return of gentleness.

Fenêtre, qu'on cherche souvent
pour ajouter à la chambre comptée
tous les grands nombres indomptés
que la nuit va multipliant.

Fenêtre, où autrefois était assise
celle qui, en guise de tendresse,
faisait un lent travail qui baisse
et immobilise. . .

Fenêtre, dont une image bue
dans la claire carafe germe.
Boucle qui ferme
la vaste ceinture de notre vue.

VII

Window we so often look for
to add to the calculated room
all the wild high numbers
night will multiply.

Window where once, disguised
as tenderness, a woman
sat doing a slow job
that debased, immobilized . . .

Window where an image sipped
from the clear carafe grows.
Buckle that can close
the vast circle of our sight.

VIII

Elle passe des heures émues
appuyée à sa fenêtre,
toute au bord de son être,
distraite et tendue.

Comme les lévriers en
se couchant leurs pattes disposent,
son instinct de rêve surprend
et règle ces belles choses

que sont ses mains bien placées.
C'est par là que le reste s'enrôle.
Ni les bras, ni les seins, ni l'épaule,
ni elle-même ne disent: assez!

VIII

She spends anxious hours
leaning on her windowsill,
tense and distracted,
on the edge of her soul.

Like greyhounds arranging
their legs as they lie down,
her dreaming instinct conquers
and rules these beautiful things

that are her well-placed hands.
That's when the rest enlists.
Neither arms, nor shoulders, nor breasts,
nor her very self can say: enough!

IX

Sanglot, sanglot, pur sanglot!
Fenêtre, où nul ne s'appuie!
Inconsolable enclos,
plein de ma pluie!

C'est le trop tard, le trop tôt
qui de tes formes décident:
tu les habilles, rideau,
robe du vide!

IX

Sigh, sigh, pure sigh!
Sill where no one leans!
Inconsolable space
full of my rain!

Your shape determines
what's too soon or too late:
you dress them up, curtain,
vestment of the void!

X

C'est pour t'avoir vue
penchée à la fenêtre ultime,
que j'ai compris, que j'ai bu
tout mon abîme.

En me montrant tes bras
tendus vers la nuit,
tu as fait que, depuis,
ce qui en moi te quitta,
me quitte, me fuit. . . .

Ton geste, fut-il la preuve
d'un adieu si grand,
qu'il me changea en vent,
qu'il me versa dans le fleuve?

X

It's because I saw you
leaning out the ultimate
window that I knew
and drank my whole abyss.

Showing me your arms
stretched toward night,
you made what was in
me that escaped you escape
me, since, and run . . .

Was your one gesture
proof of a goodbye so grand
that it turned me into wind
and dropped me in the river?

XI

Assiette verticale qui nous sert
la pitance qui nous poursuit,
et la trop douce nuit
et le jour, souvent trop amer.

L'interminable repas,
assaisonné de bleu—,
il ne faut pas être las
et se nourrir par les yeux.

Que de mets l'on nous propose
pendant que mûrissent les prunes;
ô mes yeux, mangeurs de roses,
vous allez boire la lune!

XI

Vertical plate serving us
the pittance that pursues
us, the night too tender
and day too often bitter.

Endless meal
seasoned with blue—
we just can't loll
and let our eyes feed us.

What menus are proposed
during the ripening of prunes;
O my eyes, devourers of roses,
you will drink the moon!

XII

Ce jour je suis d'humeur fenestrière,
rien que de regarder me semble vivre.
Tout me surprend d'un goût complémentaire,
d'intelligence plein comme dans un livre.

Chaque oiseau qui de son vol traverse
mon étendue, veut que je consente.
Et je consens. La force inconstante
ne m'épouvante plus, car elle me berce.

Me trouvera-t-on lorsque la nuit abonde
ayant passé le jour entier peut-être
livré à toi, inépuisable fenêtre,
pour être l'autre moitié du monde.

XII

Today I'm in a window mood,
to live seems just to look,
astonished by the better taste
of all, the fuller insight of a book.

Every bird that flies within
my reach wants me to consent.
I consent. Such an inconstant
force doesn't surprise me now, it soothes.

And when night falls, who knows,
perhaps I'll find I've spent all day
given to you, inexhaustible window,
to be the other half of the world.

XIII

Ce jour elle fut d'humeur fenestrière:
rien que de regarder lui semblait vivre.
Elle vit venir, d'inexistence ivre,
un monde à son cœur complémentaire.

On aurait dit que son regard arrose
abondamment un doux jardin d'images;
était-ce liberté ou esclavage
de ne pas changer l'indolente pose?

Son cœur, loin de ce qui vit et vire,
semblait un nombre qui soudain s'éclaire
pareil à la Balance ou la Lyre;
un presque-nom d'absences millénaires.

XIII

She was in a window mood that day:
to live seemed no more than to stare.
From a dizzy non-existence she could see
a world coming to her completing heart.

She seemed to be profusely watering
a garden of tender images with her glance;
is it liberty or slavery
not to change the pose of indolence?

Far from what's living and spinning, her heart
was a number struck by sudden brilliance
like a Balance or a Lyre;
an almost-name from ancient absences.

XIV

D'abord, au matin, petite fenêtre farouche,
au cinquième, tu te fais presque bouche,
et tu montres usées et exsangues
toutes les langues de la chambre. Ces langues
que notre vain va–et–vient fane et ronge
comme si nous étions leurs grands mensonges.
Aussi on les bat, ces langues, on les punit
de nous avoir dits et toujours redits:
Ô très-indécente descente de lit!

XIV

Tiny untamed window on the fifth,
right at dawn you turn into a mouth
of sorts, revealing all your room's
bloodless, battered tongues, tongues our
vain comings-and-goings toss and devour
as if we were their enormous lies.
We also beat these tongues, we chastise
them for having said and said and said:
Oh, how obscene that scene of falling into bed!

XV

Depuis quand nous te jouons
avec nos yeux, fenêtre!
Comme la lyre, tu devais être
rendue aux constellations!

Instrument tendre et fort
de nos âmes successives,
arrache enfin de nos sorts
ta forme définitive!

Monte! Tourne de loin
autour de nous qui te fîmes.
Soyez, astres, les rimes
trouvées à nos bouts de destin!

XV

Window, just how long have we
played you with our eyes!
Like the lyre, you should be
one of the constellations!

Tender and strong instrument
of our successive souls,
tear out your permanent
form at last from our fates.

Climb! And from afar
spin around us who created you.
Be the rhyme, O star,
found at the end of our end.

Translator's Note

The first ten of these poems were originally published in *Les Fenêtres* (1927). Poems III, IX and XI, however, originally had been included in Rilke's other sequence, *Vergers*, published in 1926.

Poems XII and XIII are from Rilke's notebooks (1921–1926). While they are ostensibly two versions of the same poem, it seems rather clear they ultimately turned out to be two entirely different poems.

Poems XIV and XV are also from Rilke's notebooks and are preceded by Rilke's notation "D'Un Cycle: 'Fenêtres'."

Although these last four poems were excluded from the sequence published in 1926, at one time or another they obviously were conceived as being part of it. That is why I am including them here.